MANAGEMENT GUIDE FOR EXECUTIVES

RAM CHANDRA CHOUDHARY

INDIA · SINGAPORE · MALAYSIA

Notion Press

No.8, 3rd Cross Street,
CIT Colony, Mylapore,
Chennai, Tamil Nadu – 600004

First Published by Notion Press 2020
Copyright © Ram Chandra Choudhary 2020
All Rights Reserved.

ISBN 978-1-64919-927-0

CONTENTS

A Few Words before You Proceed

The book will be a privilege to serve all sections of managers.

Even to those who desire to enter as management studies trainees, mid-level managers or leaders, this will add and help in achieving proven skills/knowledge which will contribute towards the accomplishment of goals.

For each individual, there are some points to be adopted for crystal-clear benefits.

I have tried to put together learnings from studies, experience, dealing with students, managers and leaders in India and abroad. I have also added knowledge gathered from educational institutions and industries. These reflect in the book from place to place.

If this book brings some change and helps in acquiring your goal, that will be my real pleasure.

Hope you like this, and in return, I get satisfaction.

– Ram Chandra Choudhary

1

Personal Behaviour

With good behaviour, you cannot exercise monetary power, but you can win millions of hearts in life.

The world is full of nice people. If you cannot find one, be one.

"Three sources of human behaviour are

  i) Desire

  ii) Emotion

  iii) Knowledge "

– Plato.

The following goes without saying:

Air, water, light, breathing, sleep, peace, pleasure from the bottom of the heart are free for all mankind. Do not make efforts to personalize these for your use only. You use these to live and let others also live.

"The richest wealth is wisdom.

The strongest weapon is patience.

The best security is faith.

The greatest tonic is laughter, and all are free for you.

Adopt them to make your life blissful.

Accept bad mistakes and bad deeds fast. A path of more delay will create a difficult path of return.

Ego, mind, logic are being followed by commas and go on, but soon you realize that it is a mistake, ask for forgiveness, eliminate commas and put a full stop then and there.

In the case of gloomy days, do not remain lost forever; rather, stand up to overcome it and proceed.

Laugh the bad days out, as even tears do not get a place in eyes.

You have to keep in mind that "**Winners are not people who never fail but people who never quit.**"

Ego is just like dust in your eyes; remove it and see the world clearly.

In one of the Indian sacred books called Mahabharat, after the events of the gambling incident, Bhishm Pitamah tells Arjun that Duryodhan is like a pitcher lying inverted on the ground, where there is space but no way to pour water (meaning wisdom).

Keep your ears open to the good advice of your close well-wishers.

"One of the greatest diseases is to be nobody to anybody."

– Mother Teresa

Do not allow too many glories to overpower you, because--

"If you are sleeping on flowers, it will be your first night, and

If flowers are sleeping over you, it will be your last night."

If you desire that the sun always shines over you, it may not be good for you.

"Sunshine all the time makes a desert." – An Arabic proverb

Never be too proud;

Never be too bossy.

You can

"Look back and get experiences,

Look forward and see hopes,

Look around and see the reality of the world,

And look within and see yourself."

Go through this case:

I was executing one part of a petrochemical project job in 2011 at Panipat on behalf of a German company. One day, I had to visit the resident construction manager in his office. Taking his permission, I entered and conveyed my point. When I was about to go out, a director of Toyo Engineering, who was present there, got up and said, "Sir, you were a fierce person when you were doing the project job in Assam. How come you have taken a U-turn now?"

I smiled and told him there was no pathway ahead.

You cannot change the world, so change yourself.

The behaviours which will help you and your organization are:

- Being active and ambitious
- Being very careful
- Being conscientious: taking time to do things right
- Creativity: can make up things easily or think of new things
- Curiosity
- Being logical
- Being organized
- Perfectionism
- Precision
- Being sober: serious, sensible or solemn

Negative behaviours include:

- Carelessness
- Impatience
- Laziness
- Rigidity
- Inattentiveness and forgetfulness
- Performing work quickly and carelessly
- Lack of discipline

Relationship-oriented behaviours:

"All of us know how to make relations, but few of us know how to maintain it," said a senior person.

The following refers to how you express opinions, handle disagreements or build connections.

Positive relationship-oriented behaviours may be described as:

- Having selfless concern for others
- Caring
- Sympathetic or concerned for others
- Considerate: thinks of others
- Faithful
- Impartial
- Pleasant
- Polite
- Sincere

Negative relationship-oriented behaviours may be described as:

- Aggressive: verbally or physically threatening.
- Argumentative.
- Bossy.
- Deceitful: doing or saying anything to get people to do what you want or to get what you want.
- Constantly trying to control others.
- Unstable and unreliable.
- Being inconsiderate.
- Manipulative.
- Seeking revenge: hurting others because you didn't get what you want.

Avoid such negative behaviours.

Words that describe introverted behaviour are:

Shy

Cowardly

Hard-headed

Indifferent

Backwards-looking

Hostile

Vociferous

These need to be shifted to positive behaviours.

Extroverted behaviour refers to actions intended to achieve gratification from external factors.

Extroverted behaviours include:

- Amiable: displays pleasant and friendly manners.

- Assertive.

- Authoritative: commanding and self-confident.

- Charismatic: shows a compelling charm that inspires devotion in others.

- Enthusiastic.

- Fond of company, sociable.

- Persuasive.

- Confident in one's character.

Extroverts are comfortable being the centre of attention, which is a prerequisite for any leadership position.

> "Difference in human being and being human is to be understood."
>
> – Ratan Tata

These will be helpful when you are dealing with group behaviour:

> "When you want to work fast, work alone,
>
> When you want to walk fast, walk together."
>
> – Ratan Tata

Have an open mind, because the mind and umbrella are both useful when open.

Sometimes, you face slide downs in your progress; learn from that and get up.

Think of basketball; falling down is not always losing.

To manage in life:

"Be honest when in trouble.

Be simple when in wealth.

Be polite when in authority.

Be silent when in anger."

Life will bring happiness, friends and prosperity if you move always in the shadow of good behaviour.

If you want to shine and remain spotless, keep your critics near you with respect.

"Hard and rigid is glass, which breaks very fast."

Adopt a flexible and sympathetic nature.

"The feet will take you to temples, but your behaviour will take you to souls, and even a child will smile with you."

Life is best for those who are enjoying it, difficult for those who are comparing it and the worst for those who are criticizing it.

"The more you praise and celebrate your life, the more there is in life to celebrate."

– Oprah Winfrey

2

MOTIVATION

The word motivation is connected to motive.

Motives are expressions of personal needs. These needs are of three types:

   i) Biological/psychological, being primary motives.

   ii) Social/psychological, being secondary motives.

   iii) Stimulating motives.

All these are a reason for doing something.

Although desire does not imply love, it does provide a motive for love.

Doing something is always about the satisfaction of motives.

The famous Harvard example is of two boys fighting for an orange; one wants the peel for baking a cake and the other wants the fruit for juice. Both fight for the orange, but their motives are different.

To consider which motive is to be satisfied first and which ones thereafter, let us look at Maslow's Hierarchy of Needs, which is as follows:

1. "All humans acquire a similar set of motives, through genetic endowment and social interaction.

2. Some motives are more basic or critical than others.

3. The more basic motives must be satisfied to a minimum level before other motives are activated.

4. As the basic motives become satisfied, the more advanced motives come into play."

This also highlights that our primary motives are essentially satisfied first and then the need for fulfilment of secondary motives is activated.

In motivation, we have to initiate a process that is target-oriented behaviour, which is a driving force behind human action.

In motivation, when you guide/apprize or stimulate a person, his motives and action trajectory change. He then follows the right path, and his approach to life turns from negative to a positive direction.

Motivation can help in improving efficiency, ways of taking action, help in eliminating addiction, increase overall well-being and happiness.

The characteristics of motivators are:

1. Personal and internal feelings for the good of the person under motivation.

2. Art of stimulating someone.

3. Produces targets.

4. Sees both the negative and positive approach of the person involved.

5. Is system-oriented.

6. It takes a lot of negotiation and bargaining to motivate.

The person who is to be the motivator and desires systematic improvement should remember the following:

i) Involve others.

ii) Visualize the rewards.

iii) Break down your targets.

iv) Feel satisfied with your achievement.

v) Review your progress.

Basically, motivations are of the following two types:

1. Extrinsic motivation, which comes from the outside, such as rewards and reinforcers like money, praise, awards, recognition and other benefits.

2. Intrinsic motivation, which comes from within, such as doing a puzzle, serving the downtrodden and the needy. It is the internal rewards like joy, relief, achievement, sense of competence and reassurance.

Some thinkers have added motivation against addiction, such as leaving unhealthy and toxic habits, improving upon the approach towards shame, guilt, withdrawal, anxiety about losing particular activities.

In addition, some minor aspects which can be improved through motivation are:

1. Incentive-based motivation - the person being motivated sees that there will be a reward ahead.

2. Fear-based motivation - teaches accountability to the person.

3. Achievement-based motivation - gives internal satisfaction to the person.

4. Power-based motivation - energizes others to take more control.

5. Affiliation-based motivation - gives recognition in the society and institute.

6. Competence-based motivation - guides to improve competence.

7. Attitude-based motivation - brings improvement in the attitude of a person.

After you get motivated, make it a habit to keep going.

"Motivation is what gets you started. Habit is what keeps you going."

— Jim Ryun

"Be miserable. Or motivate yourself. Whatever has to be done, it's always your choice."

— Wayne W. Dyer

A motivator can bring "endless hope" to a person who needs motivation and is sinking in "hopeless end".

The person who motivates an individual and brings him/her up the ladder of progress is blessed and in return learns a lot for their own improvement.

3

TARGET SETTING (PLANNING)

For any project, personal, social, educational and industrial objectives, there has to be planning which is based on the fact that all activities have to meet a targeted point of accomplishment.

Without setting a target, it will transpire as if we are taking a sleepwalk through life with no clear idea of what we want.

Targets and plans are interdependent.

"A target without a plan is just a wish."

Target setting is the first step towards our future plan.

Targets (Goals), as defined by Latham & Locke (2002), are "*the object or aim of an action, for example, to attain a specific standard of proficiency, usually within a specified time limit.*"

If a target is not set, no project will be complete, no industry will produce, no institute will function, and chaos will set in. Today, there are sophisticated planning software tools which take care of the smallest activities while making a target.

Be happy but not satisfied. Even on a personal level, you must plan your everyday work in the morning and execute it.

The first step to target setting is to decide exactly what you want. What do you want to accomplish? Then, try to get the best available information related to the goal.

"We are drowning in information but starved for knowledge."

– John Naisbitt

So, for target setting, assimilate all the information on the subject, select the best by elimination process and apply it while carrying the process for the final target setting, defining the steps of accomplishment. These steps may lead you to a larger achievement in due course of time.

In September 2006, I was working in an engineering and construction company based at Powai, Mumbai. The number of work orders was 24 to 25 and the value was between Rs 1 Cr and Rs 25 Cr each. One day, while discussing with the MD, I asked him, "Why not target projects of value of around Rs 100 Cr each because the management invests almost the same time for each work order, whether small or big." There was silence for two minutes. Then, the MD suggested, "To start with, let us target each project of Rs 50 Cr." We proceeded with this target, and recently, the company completed a work order worth Rs 1800 Cr in one of the PSU petrochemical projects on the western coast of India.

After analysing the current and attainable resources, set a time-bound ambitious target.

You have to take an action which is well thought, keeping in mind the saying "**Look before you leap.**"

Before setting the target, analyse twice or thrice and then set it. Having set it, do not look back; otherwise, you will not reach the solution.

Take the example of a student selecting a thesis topic for his research paper for PG final examination. After some weeks, he finds it difficult and selects another topic, leaving behind the first. Again, after some time, he starts wavering. Now he ends up nowhere and forgets the fact that--

"Time and tide wait for no man."

Success eludes him every moment. Such cases happen every year in large numbers. Select the topic with a good pre-plan, based on your information and guide's suggestion. Start with determination to complete it and then do it, avoiding such recurrences.

"It always seems impossible until it's done."

– Nelson Mandela.

For setting your target, consider the following:

i) It should be value-based.

ii) It should be motivating to achieve the goal.

iii) It should have a high priority in your life.

iv) It will require your sincere commitment.

v) Adopt a 'MUST DO' attitude.

vi) Write down as to why it is important for your life.

Somebody has used the word SMART at 'Linda.com' to define the requirements of target setting as:

"Any goals you set should be SMART—

(S) specific,

(M) measurable,

(A) achievable,

(R) relevant,

(T) time-bound.

These goal-setting principles improve the team's understanding of what they have to deliver, and ensure that they are able to track the progress."

The goal needs to align with your career. It should be specifically fixing the target or where you want to end up.

Locke and Latham described these five principles of target setting:

1. Clarity - A clear goal is easier to measure.

2. Challenge - One should set challenging goals. Gives specificity of targets.

3. Commitment - Team members to take up the job with personal ownership with a high level of diligence.

4. Feedback - Is essential for course correction and gives self-confidence.

5. Task complexity - Some goals require more complexity to be overcome and indicates the degree of goal demands.

Once the target is set, implementation needs to be on the fast track because:

> "Even if you are on the right track, you will get run over if you just sit there."
>
> –Will Roger.

Ensure that the job is not hampered at any time because of resources. Make a short-term and long-term action plan by writing down the individual steps to follow. Make a review schedule, maybe daily or weekly for short-term plans and monthly for long-term plans, so that you are aware as to where you are and what corrective actions are to be taken for the progress to be on the right track, leading to the achievement of the final target.

4

TIME MANAGEMENT

Time is the essence of all activities being undertaken all through life. It plays an equally important role whether you are an educationist, a businessman, a scientist, an industrialist or an enthusiastic individual in any walk of life.

A project loses its charm if time is extended beyond an acceptable limit. Disasters have taken place when an aeroplane has exceeded the time limit while landing. Relations have fizzled out when more time is taken in a settlement.

For time management, you should:

1. Make a priority list of tasks.

2. Define start to end, sequential steps.

3. Prepare and organize the tasks beforehand.

4. Always have a schedule of tasks and proceed as per the plan.

Remember that "**A job takes the time which is alloted to it reasonably.**

1. Use the idea of delegation of tasks wherever essential.

2. Stop intentionally putting off doing the tasks which can be done.

3. Avoid nonessential tasks.

4. Do not take up a number of different tasks beyond your limit. Concentrate on one to accomplish. If you have a number of

tasks to do simultaneously, have separate skilled groups, each one handling one task out of multiple tasks which are to be completed, under your regular reviewal and control.

5. Also, keep the Pareto Principle in mind: "80% of success comes from 20% of tasks."

For time management, you are managing the events in your life, where the availability is only 86,400 seconds/day. You have to develop skills through self-analysis, planning, evaluation, studies and self-control to keep the overall requirement of time within the limit.

People who practice good time management techniques often find that they:

- Are more productive.
- Have more energy for things they need to accomplish.
- Feel less stressed.
- Are able to do the things they want.
- Get more things done.

Management thinkers have said:

"Time is money."

– Benjamin Franklin

"We may delay today, but time will not."

– Benjamin Franklin

"Until we can manage, we can manage nothing."

– Peter F Drucker

"Never let yesterday use up today."

– Richard H Nelson

In Leicester, Britain, in 1987, my friend Peter was to visit me at the Penguin Hotel at 9.30 am on a Sunday. I observed that stormy wind was blowing and thick drizzles were continuing from 8.45 am. I was sure he could not come, but to my surprise, the hotel room bell rang right at 9.30 am, and Peter was there.

"Better three hours too soon than a minute too late."

– William Shakespeare

Time passes by; you have to act along with it.

"The bad news is time flies. The good news is you are the pilot."

– Michael Altshuler

To reduce time spent, move jobs together, which can be parallelly processed with the required number of capable groups.

Take care of both schedule and time because--

"While planning, tie-up schedule and time together."

– CR Chandra

"When life is full of pins and pricks, with a cool mind, ask time to put ointment over all wounds."

– CR Chandra.

Manage the PRESENT fully today because TOMORROW, namely the FUTURE, is dependent on this.

"Do not think of the past. The only thing that matters is the everlasting present."

– W. Somerset Maugham

While planning, watch out and define steps carefully because–

"For rise, it takes decades, but for fall, it takes a moment only."

Till 2016-2017, Jet Airways was the largest airline in India. Our offices were side by side in Andheri. I had observed how it had come up in the last two and a half decades, from 2 aircrafts to 134 aircrafts. I am amused by seeing it coming to a grounding halt; their shiny office with high-fliers and swanky cars is deserted, and you can see 3-4 watchmen with bamboo sticks. It could have been saved with a better plan and timely action when the financial status started dwindling beyond the acceptable limit.

> "It is not enough to be busy; so are the ants. The question
> is: What are we busy about?"
>
> – Henry David Thoreau.

Shubhyas shighram are Sanskrit words which mean if something is auspicious, do it now.

Once, while in my office, I saw 10 labour union representatives seeking permission to barge in. I called them in. They said, "We want telephones in our residences as officers have got." I told them, "It is need-based. I can give five telephones." Then they agreed to seven telephones. They went back to work. Within an hour, all telephones were operational. Their wives were asking them, "How are you?" At the end of the shift, they barged in again and told me, "We never imagined it can happen so soon. We came to thank you." I listened patiently, and with their good wishes, I saw them off.

> "Do it fast to keep the test; otherwise, it will deteriorate
> with the passage of time."
>
> – CR Chandra

Do not leave today's job for tomorrow because--

> "Tomorrow never comes."

> "While we are postponing, life speeds by."
>
> – Seneca.

Move with time, fix priority and be punctual.

"To survive, change after change.

To succeed, change with change.

To lead, cause change."

"Son, you will be old enough to do everything you like. But by then, you will be too tired to like anything."

– Glasbergen

Once, I was travelling in the north-east of India and reached the foothill of a sacred temple at 2 pm. My plane from Guwahati to Delhi was at 4 pm. I insisted to the driver to take me to the temple. There was a crowd at the temple. but a priest helped and took me inside the cave, where I had a glimpse of the worship spot. After that, I came out and asked the driver to rush. When I got out of the car at the departure entry point, an officer took me hurriedly to check-in and then inside the plane. I saw 171 angry passengers on board; they were looking furiously at me. Then, I realized the awful mistake: I was late and could not imagine the misery of the fellow passengers.

Sometimes, a delay by an individual harms the people around him/her.

"The trouble is, you think you have time."

– Jack Kornfield, *Buddha's Little Instruction Book*

"Time is not the main thing. It is the only thing."

– Miles Davis.

Put your **project** in the centre of a triangle and controlling factors like **time, cost** and **quality** one each on the apexes. It becomes a perfect project triangle. Now, see a case where time is ballooning, and then observe what happens to project accomplishment and the consequent cost and quality.

Make a list of jobs to be done by you every morning, before starting the work. Divide your jobs into A, B, C priorities and pay more attention to A category of jobs over the day, while the other two are also to be attended to. Review at the end of the day regularly.

If you are the boss, get the task done by your subordinates as per their job allocation because the job will be accomplished not only by your two hands but will be done by hundreds and thousands of hands behind you. Do not forget periodical reviews or getting feedback at the closing hours of the day, to keep the job completion time under control.

5

STRESS MANAGEMENT

Stress occurs when you perceive that the demands placed on you—such as work, school or relationship—exceed your capability to cope.

Effective stress management helps you break the hold that stress has on your life, so you can be happier, healthier and more productive. The ultimate goal is a balanced life, with time for work, relationships and relaxation.

Some stresses can be beneficial at times, producing a boost that can provide the necessary drive and energy to overcome a challenge.

"A person becomes poor, not because of less earning but because of unending aspirations."

You will have stress mainly from **politics**, **money** and **work**.

You always see people up the ladder, and your desire forces you to stretch up there; then you start wondering how the stress has crept up in you.

A boy used to fight daily with his father for a pair of new shoes, as his classmates in school had the same. The father was unable to manage. One evening, while walking, the boy saw a person below a tree. The person had no legs. The boy returned to his father and said, "Papa, for me, the sandals are all right. I do not require shoes."

Keep your wishes within your means with a cool sense of satisfaction.

We are worried about our failures and mistakes.

"Anyone who has never made a mistake has never tried anything new."

– Albert Einstein

"Don't worry about failures, worry about the chances you miss when you don't even try."

– Jack Canfield.

Albrechts has defined stresses as:

i) Time stress

ii) Anticipatory stress

iii) Situational stress and

iv) Encounter for stress.

When you are highly stressed:

"To reduce stress, come down on your desires."

– Swami Chinmayananda

If you cannot handle stress, you cannot handle success.

Do not stress yourself out; believe that the situation will change.

To reduce stress, avoid:

• Smoking • Drinking too much • Overeating or undereating • Zoning out for hours in front of the TV or computer • Withdrawing from friends, family and activities • Using pills or drugs to relax • Sleeping too much • Do not try offloading your stress on others.

Instead, you should:

- Take a 10-minute walk. According to a few experts, if you take a walk, it will help reduce endorphins in the system that cause stress.

- Practice mindfulness. Learning to focus on your breathing can help you reduce stress.

- Maintain a positive attitude.

- Accept that there are events that you cannot control.

- Be assertive instead of aggressive. Assert your feelings, opinions or beliefs instead of becoming angry, defensive or passive.

- Learn and practice relaxation techniques; try meditation, yoga.

- Exercise regularly.

- Eat balanced meals.

- Learn to manage your time more effectively.

- Set limits appropriately and learn to say no to requests that would create excessive stress in your life.

- Make time for hobbies, interests and relaxation.

- Get enough rest and sleep, to recover from stressful events.

- Don't rely on alcohol or drugs to reduce stress.

- Seek out social support.

- Some sources of stress are unavoidable. If you can't prevent or change them, accept things as they are.

- Don't try to control the uncontrollable.

- Share your feelings or talk to a trusted friend.

- Learn to forgive. Free yourself from negative energy by forgiving and moving on.

- If you can't change the stressor, change yourself. You can adapt to stressful situations and regain your sense of control by changing your expectations and attitude.

- Look at the big picture. Will the stressful situation change in a month or a year? Then focus your time and energy elsewhere.

- Perfectionism is a major source of avoidable stress. Set reasonable standards for yourself and others, and sometimes, learn to be okay with "good enough".

- Focus on the positive side. Adjust your attitude from negative thoughts.

Once, I was under stress due to a change in the boss; he had his own whims, fancies and preferences for one as compared to other employees. One of my seniors advised me, "You keep on doing your job sincerely and forget everything else." I did that with some more efforts.

The last stage of annual report writing is moderation of the report by the top authority and HODs for particular grades. I expected adverse remarks from my new boss. Once, I met another HOD, for whom I had a lot of respect. When I told him that the person might have given adverse appraisal for me, he said, "In the last review, when the top official asked all the bosses 'who is the best in this particular grade in the operating factory?' The same fellow gave your name and added 'who else?'"

Then, he advised, "You have told me, but do not tell anybody else because **walls have ears**."

Believe in your performance, remain confident and proceed further with all sincerity.

In a stressful condition, accept the unavoidable stressor and do your best.

"When none speaks for you, your work will speak."

In a stressful situation, follow these 4 As:

i) Avoid – Avoid stressors; maybe reduce unimportant work. Avoid causes of stress by reducing the time you spend with them.

ii) Alter – If it's not avoidable, change the way you operate.

iii) Adopt – Adaption of stress if it's unavoidable and unalterable.

iv) Accept – If it's unavoidable/unalterable/unadoptable, accept the situation and proceed.

If the stress is pressing more, sit for a while in a twilight area, remember that in past you have seen the waterfall, the flowery garden, the green mountain, the cloudy sky, the seashore tides, the innocent lovely child, the showering love of your friend, and if you believe in God, remember your God and relax.

6

SWOT ANALYSIS

To proceed on the right path, you should know your strengths, weaknesses, opportunities and threats. Analyse these to know beforehand so that you are prepared for any eventuality. Think of which quality you can pursue and which you can hold on to. Make efforts to improve on the qualities from negative to positive before you think of using these. Make your efforts continuously to achieve your target within your limit as per your SWOT analysis.

To analyse, write the facts in four quadrants of a rectangle; 1st Qtr - Strengths, 2nd Qtr - weaknesses, 3rd Qtr - Opportunities and 4th Qtr - Threats. In each quarter, write the relevant qualities you possess and then decide on your move. Some of the qualities have been mentioned ahead point-wise for reference.

Sometimes, you may have to take risks because there is a saying, "NO RISK, NO GAIN." But this should be an analysed and calculated risk. You may have to take some pain in the bargain.

"Pain is temporary. Quitting lasts forever."

– Lance Armstrong.

In this world, numerous dreams have been broken due to the habit of thinking 'what people will say'. Do not be afraid of others as long as you are clear in your SWOT analysis and are marching ahead with confidence.

Remove I, M from the word IMPOSSIBLE and then you say, "I can do it. It is POSSIBLE."

"You think you finished, but the flight is still due.

You finished the ground, but the sky is still due."

F.E.A.R has two meanings:

1. Forget Everything And Run

2. Face Everything And Rise

The meaning of three Fs related to Fear, Flight & Fight:

For success, you have to fight fear, as flight from fear will result in losing the complete game.

Do not underestimate your strength;

"It's not the load that brings you down, it's the way you carry it."

– Lou Holtz

"If you want to fly, give up everything that weighs you down."

– Buddha

In the term 'SWOT', each of the four letters describes one word given here in four parts:

Strengths

Strength means positive attributes, tangible and intangible, internal to you and your organization within your control.

What internal resources do you have? Think about the following:

i) Positive attributes of people, such as knowledge, background, education, credentials, network, reputation or skills.

ii) Tangible assets of the company, such as capital, credit, existing customers, distribution channels, patents or technology.

iii) What advantages do you have over your competitors? Such as R&D, manufacturing, logistics facilities, better-skilled manpower.

iv) Other internal aspects that add value or offer you a competitive advantage.

Weaknesses

These are the aspects of your business that place you in a competitive disadvantage.

i) Look for and maintain your competitive edge.

ii) Bring improvement to accomplish your objectives, compete with your environment and place adequate skilled manpower, money, material, logistics and other required resources.

Opportunities

These are external attractive factors:

i) New additions of technology, revamp, renovation to improve output.

ii) Market innovations.

iii) Government providing a new opening in business.

Threats

Threats are external factors beyond your control. Take care of

i) Competitors and have your contingency plans.

ii) Forces beyond your control.

iii) Unfavourable trend in your market, revenues and profits.

iv) Changes pertaining to your inputs.

v) Change in economy, regulation of the country.

vi) Change in technology, any impending agitation/calamities.

Remodel your resources to supplement your job.

Enhance your facilities so that you can meet the theme of the proverb "Cut your coat according to your cloth."

Use SWOT analysis as an add-on tool while you are making a plan for achieving your goal.

7

KNOWLEDGE-BUILDING

Today, knowledge has been built up, documented and catalogued to an unimaginable scale. Knowledge has been built up since time immemorial. National/international libraries/bookstalls/software and hardware gadgets are storing these large volumes on a variety of subjects. This knowledge is also available subject-wise in the mind of learned scholars present in the world. One wonders how different countries' authors' knowledge of different subjects are available in documents all over and are available to people who really desire to refer to them.

As aspirants of knowledge, let us go through the following thinkers' statements:

Knowledge is like a garden; if it is not cultivated, it cannot be harvested.

"Knowledge is life with wings."

– William Blake

"There is no wealth like knowledge, no poverty like ignorance."

– Buddha

"Knowledge with action converts adversity into prosperity."

– A.P.J. Abdul Kalam

Knowledge-building is the process of creating, sharing, using and preserving the knowledge and information of an individual or an organization. It refers to a multidisciplinary approach to achieve organizational objectives by making the best use of knowledge.

"To attain a higher level of knowledge, add things every day."

You get initial knowledge from your family, then educational institutions and subsequently by working in industries, institutions, various establishments and businesses.

During my childhood, I used to hear that there was a person from a poor family in a nearby village who became an engineer. Since then, I was determined to get the same education. I worked for it and did BE. I got a job in a large PSU in Sindri, which was near the institution where I did BE. Here, while at work, in my spare moments, I started doing ME in mechanical engineering, machine design and got success. Later, I shifted to a PSU (one of the three large oil PSUs) in Mumbai, and from there, in the same way, I completed Master of Administrative Management from JBIMS (BOM. Univ.). The journey was extremely strenuous, but I had the determination to collect knowledge and apply it in the industries.

That determination was always guiding me ahead, and I was following its shadow sincerely.

"Wisdom is not a product of schooling but of the lifelong attempt to acquire it."

– Albert Einstein.

To enrich wisdom, distribute your knowledge regularly.

Knowledge management efforts typically focus on organizational or individual objectives such as improved performances, success in competitions/research while sharing the information gained, and its integration brings upgradation of the organization or individual's capability.

Knowledge management is an enabler of organizational learning.

A lot of efforts are required for improving knowledge management for self and the organization

"Genius is 1% inspiration and 99% perspiration."

– Thomas Edison

" I can is 100 times more important than IQ."

– Albert Einstein."

Learn by experience acquired in the field of your prime interest.

"Knowledge is power? No. Knowledge on its own is nothing, but the application of useful knowledge, now that is powerful."

– Rob Liano

"Ideas are in the air like invisible seeds and they drift into our minds every day."

– Robert E. Mueller

My friend, the then CMD of Hindustan Diamond Company at Atlanta Building in Nariman Point, once took me to the strong room and showed me raw diamonds. I was not happy to see the stones. Then, he took me to the strong room of polished diamonds, kept in glass selves, and all the lights were turned on by the treasurer, The room was dazzling, and my eyes were amused.

Then, he added, "When knowledge of cutting and polishing is applied, then only the whole world recognizes the real importance of a diamond."

There are many well-defined criteria for different quotients:

i) PQ (Personal Quotients)

Keep up with food, exercise, rest and sleep.

ii) IQ (Intelligence Quotient)

Keep it up with reasoning, problem-solving. Remain under the umbrella of perpetual learning.

iii) EQ (Empathy Quotient)

Banish anger. Think if you were in his position; care for others too.

iv) SQ (Spiritual Quotient)

Collect wealth for the better good (e.g. removal of malnutrition).

To manage knowledge-building, consider the following strategies which are needed by organizations or individuals:

- Knowledge-sharing – Bring in a culture that encourages the sharing of information, based on the concept that knowledge should be shared among employees and updated to remain relevant.
- Make knowledge-sharing a key role in employees' job description.
- Storytelling as a means of transferring knowledge.
- Cross-project learning is to be documented so as to safely retain acquired knowledge. It should be stored well so that all those who need this solution in the future can get it.
- Best practice transfer.

Competency-based management, systematic evaluation and planning of knowledge-related competency of individual organization members:

- Mentor-mentee relationship, job shadowing.
- Collaborative software technologies.
- Knowledge repositories - databases, documents library etc.

- Measuring and reporting intellectual capital - a way of making explicit knowledge for the company.

Knowledge gained during the execution of different projects, commissioning, operation and maintenance is to be gathered. Lessons learned are to be documented and catalogued for subsequent requirements. This knowledge management/collection becomes a high-value asset which can be used for guidance during problems for future execution of jobs, resulting in a large saving in time, money and manpower.

8

DECISION-MAKING

For making a decision for the benefit of an individual or an organization, first, you have to have sufficient information regarding the same. Make alternative decisions list based on the available information and choose one out of the lot, with dedication, before proceeding.

Decisions are the hardest thing to be made, especially when it is a choice between where you should be and where you want to be.

Decision-making is important not only in business, but it is also important throughout life, which moves on a series of decisions.

Let us consider some opinions of management thinkers:

"Uncertainty can lead to paralysis. And if you become indecisive, you're dead."

– Jim Citro

"Again and again, the impossible decision is solved when we see that the problem is only a tough decision waiting to be made."

– Dr Robert Schuller

"Stay committed to your decisions, but stay flexible in your approach."

– Tony Robbins

Mind that in the above decision,

> "May your choices reflect your hopes, not fear."
>
> – Nelson Mandela

> "You can't make decisions based on fear and the possibility
> of what might happen."
>
> – Michelle Obama

You have to have the courage to decide.

> "Whenever you see a successful business, someone once
> made a courageous decision."
>
> – Peter F. Drucker

> "Success is not final, failure is not fatal: it is the courage to
> continue that counts."
>
> – Winston Churchill

Take suggestions from others if you feel it's necessary while shortlisting but decide yourself; do not be dependent on others.

> "If you care about what people will think of you, you will
> end up being their slave. Reject and pull up your own rope."
>
> – Auliq Ice

The following are five different types of decision-making skills:

- Intuitive is one of the simplest and arguably one of the most common ways to make a decision.

- Rational is the type of decision-making most people want to believe they do.

- Satisfying.

- Collaborative.

- Combination of above four skills.

One can follow these 7 decision-making process steps:

1. Select and collect the probable decisions.

   First, identify the problem you need to solve. Clearly define the problem first and then your decision. Your decision is to be measurable and should project time requirement clearly, so you know for certain that you will meet the goal timely, at the end of the process.

2. Gather relevant information.

   Now, gather the information relevant to that choice. Do an internal assessment. Also, seek information from external sources, including studies, market research, and, in some cases, evaluation from paid consultants.

3. Identify the alternatives.

   With relevant information, you will find, usually, more than one option to consider when trying to meet a goal.

4. Weigh the evidence.

   Once you have identified multiple alternatives, compare these and see what companies have done in the past to succeed in these areas, and take a sincere look at your own organization's wins and losses. Identify potential pitfalls for each of your alternatives.

5. Choose among alternatives and select the best one to dwell upon.

6. Take action.

   Once you've made your decision, act on it! Develop a plan to make your decision tangible and achievable. Make a plan and set the team on their tasks once the plan is in place.

7. Review your decision which will give the correct solution.

   While following the above steps of the decision-making process, take an honest look back at your decision from time to time: Did you solve the problem? Did you answer the question? Did you meet your goals?

If so, take note of what worked, for future reference. If not, learn from your mistakes, bring in corrective measures, as you begin the decision-making process again.

While working as a junior engineer in a fertilizer plant, I was given the job of constructing 22 bunkers in their coal yard, and the time limit was 9 months. Up to 7 months, I could never meet my chief maintenance engineer. I met only some mid-managers. One day, I decided to meet him, went up to the door, had no courage to open the latch and returned after a few seconds. Thereafter, I read in a magazine that '**A man who hesitates is lost**'.

The next evening, I approached straight to the door, opened the latch and, after asking for permission, went to him. To my surprise, he was waiting to know the position. When I apprized that 20 were complete, and the remaining two bunkers would be completed by the end of the month, he was so happy. He congratulated me and took me to the general manager to inform him, who in turn appreciated me.

While taking a decision, never hesitate once you have the facts and figures with you.

You have to decide at the right time; a decision at the wrong time is useless. You have to decide faster.

"Before using, you can go on peeling the onion, but to a certain stage only."

Decide on the basis of the information you collected over a time period and--

"Let us not try and boil the ocean." Rather, think more, decide fast, as the time at your disposal is limited.

In order to have a mindset for taking faster decisions:

    i) Limit your options.

   ii) Draw a hard line between good and bad choices.

  iii) Listen to the gut feeling.

  iv) Think of that your time is money.

   v) Know that decisiveness grows with each decision.

  vi) Remember that indecisiveness kills.

A Chinese proverb says, "The best time to plant a tree was 20 years ago; the second-best time is now."

"In summer, you enjoy the shadow of a tree." But ponder and you find that it was somebody's decision to plant it, much before.

Always target a timely and well-thought decision which is taken by you and then proceed with full courage and keen efforts for execution.

9

PUBLIC SPEAKING

The first step in public speaking is the preparation of the topic in the best way.

When you desire to succeed, remember:

"Preparation comes before success, even in the dictionary."

It is the process of making a selective, intellectual judgement from available information of several complex alternatives, variables and then deciding on the course of action or idea/subject.

> "There are only three speeches, for every one you actually gave. The one you practice, the one you gave, and the one you wish you gave."
>
> – Dale Carnegie.

> "You can speak well if your tongue can deliver the message of your heart."
>
> – John Ford

Courage follows preparation.

> "Public also notices his stage fear when a wrestler is saluting and taking arena dust on his forehead before stepping in."
>
> – CR Chandra

"The best way to conquer stage fright is to know what you are talking about."

– Michael H. Mescon

How to start:

"When speaking in public, your message, no matter how important, will not be effective or memorable if you do not have a clear structure."

– Patricia Frap

So, prepare a proper structure of your topic. Write and read till you are the master of the written material, which is sequentially arranged. This will impart confidence in you.

"One important key to success is self-confidence. An important key to self-confidence is preparation."

– Arthur Ashe

Once you have prepared in the best possible way, then you speak out.

Also note: "Let the speech be better than silence or be silent."

– Dionysius of Halicarnassus

Here is a real-life event:

It was the initial stage of my service in 1975 in a large PSU at Sindri. The company organized a 6-day public speaking course at the campus by a learned guide for 40 of their engineers and managers, and I had the opportunity to participate as well.

In the beginning, the guide set two rules:

i) Every day, each participant has to speak for five minutes on the dais.

ii) Every alternate day, starting from the 1st day, he will give a topic, and from the 2nd alternate day, participants will select, prepare and then deliver their topic. On the 1st day, when speaking, one of the participants cried on stage, pulled a chair, sat and had water. But he continuously improved subsequently, and on the last day, he was speaking boldly.

I felt light tremors in my leg on the first day but could speak for five minutes. Thereafter, every day witnessed improvements because of hard preparation, good theme collections and practising the speech. The final day saw a dramatic change and the level of speech was adjudged the best. The person who had cried on the first day kept on improving, and on the last day, he gave a non-stop, interesting speech. In terms of the rate of improvement, he was adjudged to be the best.

"Prepare and practice with zeal and deliver with confidence."

To become a good speaker, follow these steps:

1. Prepare the topic well.

2. If you are a beginner, you must practice twice or thrice by speaking alone or before a mirror.

3. Address the gathering when you begin your speech.

4. Speak at a normal pace.

5. Maintain eye contact with all four quarters of the audience hall, turn by turn.

6. Use the podium and sometimes make small movements once you feel settled on the dais.

7. Even veterans review the text and practice the delivery of the speech.

8. Revise the delivery material for correction of spelling, accuracy and relatability to public demand.

9. Keep your text sequential because, generally, people miss the track while you search through papers on the dais.

10. Conclude briefly.

11. Be prepared for questions and answers.

12. Say thanks to the listeners.

Let me write about one more case here:

IOCL was celebrating their golden jubilee in 2009, in their various refineries. The function was also held in the town hall of one of their north-east refineries. The company was launching its slogan for IOCL, 'Energy of India'. I was given the opportunity to be the last guest speaker.

I prepared the speech, keeping the slogan in the centre and the total IOCL structure

around in sequence. After the speech, when I was stepping down, the VVIP

invitee came, shook my hand and congratulated me for the best speech. He added, "Each word in its right place."

Then, with a smile, we separated.

Keep in mind that your speech should have words/sentences in proper sequential order and must fit the occasion.

If you prepared well, then--

"Preparation will bring accuracy and practice will bring perfection."

When you are asked to deliver extemporal, you have to think and quickly decide bullet points while you are moving from your seat to the podium and stick to those points.

"Have courage to speak up, which can also be soft and dignified." Told to Ratan Tata by Navajbai Seth Tata, his grandmother

Look confident because you have prepared the topic better than the audience.

Learn from mistakes, and if it went well, note what made it like that.

Embrace the challenge; public speaking projects your strength to the audience.

Speak what you know well.

> "You are not being judged, the value of what you are bringing to the audience is being judged."
>
> – Seth Godin

You can keep a few copies of a brief of the presentation material as handouts.

10

LISTENING

It will be better to recognize the meaning of the word UP-NI-SAD, a religious book written in Sanskrit. If you have to listen to and get knowledge from a person, then make him sit on a higher platform (UP), go nearer to him/her (NI), then sit down there (SAD) and listen.

Knowledge will flow seamlessly from the person to you like a river flows.

> "80% of our success in learning from other people is based upon how well we listen."
>
> – Marshal Goldsmith

"The thing about listening that escapes most people is that they think of it as a passive activity. You don't have to do anything. You sit there like a lump and hear someone out.

> Not true. Good listeners regard what they do as a highly active process—with every muscle engaged, especially the brain."
>
> – Marshal Goldsmith

While listening--

> "Listen with curiosity. Speak with honesty. Act with integrity."

The greatest problem with us, during listening, is that we don't listen to understand. We listen to reply.

"When we listen with curiosity, we don't listen with the intent to reply. We listen for what's behind the words."

– Roy T. Bennett

Listen with a view to capture the topic from different sources as--

"Education isn't something you can finish."

– Isaac Asimov

Listening skills are essential to many business roles and functions, such as:

- managing, coaching, mentoring, facilitation
- sales, negotiation, arbitration, market research
- appraisal, interviewing, training, consultancy

After good listening, you can handle activities well, such as:

- making decisions
- reaching agreements
- selling and influencing
- dealing with customer complaints
- getting and giving information (such as policy, instructions, feedback, marketing information)

Here are eight quotes about the all-important skill of listening:

1. "Wisdom is the reward you get for a lifetime of listening when you'd have preferred to talk."

– Doug Larson

2. "Listening is a magnetic and strange thing, a creative force. The friends who listen to us are the ones we move toward. When we are listened to, it creates us, makes us unfold and expand."

– Karl A. Menninger

3. "Most of the successful people I've known are the ones who do more listening than talking."

– Bernard Baruch

4. "Most people do not listen with the intent to understand; they listen with the intent to reply."

– Stephen R. Covey

5. "Friends are those rare people who ask how we are, and then wait to hear the answer."

– Ed Cunningham

6. "The art of conversation lies in listening."

– Malcolm Forbes

7. "You cannot truly listen to anyone and do anything else at the same time."

– M. Scott Peck

8. "We have two ears and one tongue so that we would listen more and talk less."

– Diogenes

You have to be attentive or intuitive or appreciative towards the talk.

As per your need, focus on listening by being

1. Appreciative - While listening, your body language should reflect honour and appreciation.

2. Empathic - Give a feeling of deep-rooted belief and encourage the speaker with your facial and eye expressions while you are listening.

3. Comprehensive - Remain focused until the speech ends.

4. Critical - Listen to the ideas of the speaker attentively, ask related and genuine questions, give feedback.

Active listening

It makes sense: When it's done right, active listening—fully listening to the speaker and providing verbal and non-verbal feedback—can help you to draw people out, avoid misunderstandings, foster collaboration, settle disagreements and gain people's trust.

i) Listen at least as much as you talk

"I only wish I could find an institute that teaches people how to listen. Business people need to listen at least as much as they need to talk. Too many people fail to realize that real communication goes in both directions."

– Lee Iacocca, former president and CEO, Chrysler Corporation

ii) Never stop listening

"Of all the skills of leadership, listening is the most valuable— and one of the least understood. Most captains of industry listen only sometimes, and they remain ordinary leaders. But a few, the great ones, never stop listening. That's how they get word before anyone else of unseen problems and opportunities."

– Peter Nulty, Fortune Magazine

iii) Learn by listening

"I remind myself every morning: Nothing, I say this day will teach me anything. So if I'm going to learn, I must do it by listening."

– Larry King, TV host

iv) Listening openly and actively

"To learn through listening, practice that you listen openly, ready to learn something, as opposed to listening defensively, ready to rebut. Listening actively means you acknowledge what you heard and act accordingly."

v) Use your eyes and your ears

"If you make listening and observation your occupation, you will gain much more than you can by talk."

Good listening allows us to demonstrate that we are paying attention to the thoughts, feelings and behaviours of the other person (seeing the world through their eyes).

Listening is crucial to maintaining productive relationships, and sometimes the only way to establish communication.

During listening, avoid impatience and let the other person finish. When it's your turn to speak, give your views and ask relevant questions.

11

COMMUNICATION

Communication is conveying clearly your ideas and thoughts to others so that an effective understanding prevails on both sides without any ambiguity.

You can explain and convince the opposite person when you know your subject well.

> "If you can't explain it simply, you don't understand it well enough."
>
> – Albert Einstein

> "Information is giving out, communication is getting through."
>
> – Sydney J. Harris

Communication becomes a media for expression to establish a bond in education, business, personal, group discussion fields.

> "When the trust account is high, communication is easy, instant and effective."

One can argue with facts through soft conversation.

A well-timed positive word or compliment can change the course of someone's day.

Communication can be--

Verbal - Convey orally and listen to understand the meaning of the subject, by each other.

Written - It can be in black and white in agreeable formats.

Non-verbal - You observe a person and can infer meaning by his/her

  i) Body language

  ii) Eye contact and eye expressions

  iii) Facial expression

  iv) Touch

  v) Space

For clear communication:

"Write to be understood, speak to be heard, read to grow."
— Lawrence Clark Powell

"Nothing lowers the level of communication more than raising the voice."
— Stanley Horowitz

Top skills in communication are:

1. Preparation of what to communicate

2. Cohesion and clarity

3. Sequential flow

4. Emotional intelligence

5. Friendliness

6. Confidence

7. Empathy

8. Respect

9. Listening

10. Open-mindedness

11. Tone of voice

12. Stress management

13. Speak up with right time pause in between

14. Readiness for questions and answers

If you do not have something nice and factual to say, do not say anything at all.

'You' is the most important word in any conversation. Minimize the 'I' and the 'Me' and focus on the 'You'.

"What will they think of me? Must be put aside for bliss."

– Joseph Campbell

"I speak to everyone in the same way, whether he is the garbage man or the president of the university."

– Albert Einstein

While talking to a person, treat them with respect, no matter their status.

"Do not be embarrassed by your failures. Learn from them and start again."

– Sir Richard Branson

Miscommunications and misunderstandings happen! Do not start cursing yourself. If there is time, correct the version.

"The most important thing in communication is hearing what isn't said."

– Peter F. Drucker

The ability to read the emotions and non-verbal communication of another person increases understanding and elevates relationships.

"Wise men speak because they have something to say; fools because they have to say something."

– Plato

Speak with a purpose, not just to fill up the silence. Remember: Silence is a gift that allows self-reflection.

"The difference between the right word and almost right word is the difference between lightning and a lightning bug."

– Mark Twain

Words are powerful. When you chose just the right word, you increase understanding tenfold.

"The way we communicate with others and with ourselves ultimately determines the quality of our lives."

– Anthony Robbins

Good communication with the right theme always wins hearts, creates friends and catalyses business.

12

GROUP DISCUSSION (GD)

A group discussion assesses the personality of a person. It finds out the behavioural traits in a person, his or her leadership skills, technical skills, depth of general knowledge, social skills, team skills, problem-solving skills and presence of mind.

For a successful GD, a group of five or more than five participants are to be present.

All the group members get a chance to participate, ponder upon the ideas and reach a target solution.

This is possible with a purposeful integration, to exchange ideas, thoughts and feelings, in creating a common goal.

In management entrance examinations, it is a technique to judge the communication skills of the participants.

The skills being judged are:

1. Communication.
2. Your behaviour and interaction with the group.
3. Open-mindedness.
4. Listening skills.
5. How you put forward your views.
6. Your leadership and decision-making skills.

7. Your subject knowledge and analysis skill.

8. Your problem-solving and critical thinking skill.

9. Your attitude and confidence.

For an effective GD, these are essential:

1. A chance for all members to express their views freely and frankly.

2. Others' ideas are heard openly and feedback is received with due respect.

3. Discussion is not dominated by one person.

4. Arguments are based on ideas and concepts and not on personality.

5. Discussions are to resolve disputes, find solutions, create plans, come to a conclusion and then proceed for further deliberations.

6. Decide on the action, provide mutual support, solve problems and conflicts, and plan your work on an event.

DOs and DON'Ts

DOs

1. Appearance - formal but groomed.

2. Introduce yourself to the group humbly.

3. If you have correct primary information on the topic, then start or else listen to the speakers carefully and then make your point.

4. Speak and put forth your views.

5. Respect and encourage others' views.

6. Ask open-ended questions.

7. Control your own bias.

8. During a disagreement, help the group to use it creatively.

9. If you are having no point, you can support a member whose point is correct. It is not useful to lengthen the talk.

10. In such talks, when you have fewer points, "less is more."

11. Have a positive attitude.

12. Contribute to making sure that the discussion remains on track.

13. Speak clearly and sensibly.

DON'Ts

1. Do not be a fount of wisdom.

2. Do not try to dominate all through the discussion once you have made your point.

3. Do not support a point to override others, unless it is based on facts and figures.

Speak the right point at the right time. Many times, vociferous people lose the game.

Stay silent if you do not know the correct answer, but when you have a valid and correct answer/suggestion, speak out to the group.

13

INTERVIEW

An interview begins with your resume. It should reflect your education, experience, achievements and your important skills, including technical, IT and soft skills. Even when the help of a recruiting agency is taken, they ask for the CV first and from there the processing starts.

The soft skill in the resume should reflect the following

i) Will Power

ii) Positive attitude

iii) Dependability

iv) Resourcefulness

v) Verbal communication

vi) Listening

vii) Time management

viii) Customer care

ix) Willingness to learn and to work under pressure

x) Extracurricular activities

Apart from recruiting agencies, organizations are also adopting various methods to conduct interviews, like:

- Telephonic interview.
- Video conferencing.
- Group discussion.
- Assessment through the day, including written, case studies, GD, etc.
- Individual (face to face) interview.
- Panel interview.
- Sometimes, selected candidates also have to be finally interviewed by the CEO.

During the interview, your appearance should match the saying "The first impression is the last impression" to a reasonable extent.

Your outfit depends on what is prevalent in the other side group; generally, a suit or formal, sober outfit is preferred. A white full shirt, black full pant, a black pair of shoes for males is very often a likeable set; for females, a slightly longish, sober dress should be ok. The dress should be cleaned, pressed and comfortable for you.

Face the interview with confidence that--

"You are unrepeatable. There is a magic about you that is all your own."

– D. M. Dellinger

Further, for an interview, you must take note of the following points:

1. Review your resume before the interview.
2. Do your homework and background retrospection.

3. Be polite to everyone.

4. Watch your body language. To give the interview, you can sit straight or lean forward a bit.

5. Have eye contact with the interviewers.

6. Watch your language; do not fly bombs.

7. Prepare for standard questions.

8. Prepare your questions, maybe on challenges of the new position, your work in the new set-up.

9. Do not blame your earlier employer.

10. Do not talk too much.

11. Listen and then answer.

12. Do not forget to thank the interviewers at the end.

You should be well prepared to answer these common questions:

1. Tell us a little about yourself.

2. What is your biggest weakness?

3. What is your biggest strength?

4. Why should we hire you?

5. Why do you want to leave your current organization?

6. Why do you want this job?

7. What is your biggest professional achievement?

8. Describe your dream job.

9. Tell us the toughest decision you had to make in the last six months.

10. What was your salary in your last job?

11. What questions do you have for us?

12. What do you plan to do if you are selected here?

The end should be pleasant, and never forget to thank the interviewers.

14

NEGOTIATION

One purpose of negotiation is that each party is equally interested in the decision of the other; maybe each one is interested in more, but negotiation, in principle, is a "give and take" process.

A successful negotiation ends in finding solutions, settling differences between parties who desire to get better value, price, products, services, deals.

One major part of any successful business is an efficient negotiation.

A situation like war and conflicts is not always advisable. Mostly, a peaceful negotiation has proven to be a winning proposition.

> "Negotiation is a technique. It is something you use when it is to your advantage."
>
> – John Bolton

Listen, with patience, to the arguments from both sides before making a comment point-wise.

We have realized that during negotiations, new ideas come up with suggestions for an improved mode of operation. Negotiation brings up a mutually agreed solution and thus benefits both parties.

Take care of the following five fundamental points in negotiations, which people often neglect:

1. Prepare your brief fully.

2. Build a talented, happy and cohesive team.

3. Build a common fact base.

4. Think outside your own box, keeping both groups in mind.

5. Think win-win.

These five fundamentals have applicability to almost any negotiation you will encounter.

If you are a negotiator, then plan your strategies sequentially to succeed:

1. As homework, study the case thoroughly.

2. Pinpoint the legitimacy of your case.

3. Identify areas of agreement.

4. Get points together which probably resolve the disagreements, seek alternate solutions and introduce trade-offs.

5. Carry documents.

6. You may show your legal and valid documents across the table if required during the discussion.

While starting the process of negotiation:

1. Keep your presentation material ready, if you have any.

2. Welcome the opposite group with warmth. Extend all necessary courtesy.

3. Mould the situation such that the negotiation becomes a joint search for arriving at the solution.

4. Aim high to begin with so that you can give incentives in the end. However, give concessions reluctantly.

5. Unless it is an urgent requirement, do not disclose a 'no' in the beginning, as this is a loser's bite.

6. It is easier to resist in the beginning than at the end.

7. Finish areas of agreement first and then discuss areas of disagreement.

8. Agree without being disagreeable.

9. Break down complex deals; no emotions, deal with facts.

10. Ensure a win-win situation and use an integrative approach.

"If you want to reach an agreement, move from a competitive mindset to a cooperative one."

– Ludovic Tendron

"The best move you can make in negotiation is to think of an incentive the other person hasn't even thought of—and then meet it."

– Eli Broad

"If there is negotiation, it must be rooted in respect and concern for the rights of others."

– John F. Kennedy.

1. Summarize and ensure acceptancy

2. Always take prints with the signature of party leaders on points discussed.

As a successful negotiator, in the end, one has to note the following points:

- You should have the best alternative to a negotiated decision with you. This will be an ultimate threshold limit plan from your side that you can offer in case you fail to reach an agreement at the bargaining table with your counterpart. You try your best with the alternate proposal before you reject an offer.

- Conflict resolution

  Conflict resolution is the process of resolving a dispute or a conflict by meeting at least some of each side's needs and addressing their interests. It should not be all through one party's concern solution; rather, other's concern is also to be looked after sympathetically.

  "Good negotiation is not about getting everything your way. It is balancing each other's target."

  – David Olive

The end of negotiation has to be on a happy note for both parties. This will ultimately bring wilful concerted efforts by both groups for the accomplishment of the targeted assignment.

15

TRAINING

Contribute your experience, even in a small way, to train your colleagues and contribute the knowledge to humanity.

A candle loses nothing by lighting another candle. The more training you impart, the more knowledge gain for you is assured.

Broadly, there are three types of training:

1. New job training

2. Imparting developmental training

3. Transitional training

Methods of training:

1. Technology-based

2. Simulators-based

3. On the job training

4. Coaching, mentoring and monitoring

5. Lectures

6. Group discussions and tutorials

7. Role playing

8. Management games

9. Case studies

You can concentrate on the following topics for the training of your managers/executives:

1. Industry-specific regulations

2. Creating an inclusive workforce

3. Conflict resolution

4. Cybersecurity

5. Hiring and firing

6. Nurturing talent, coaching and employee retention

7. Emergency procedures

8. Identifying training needs

9. Accessibility requirements

10. What it means to manage

Modus operandi at the training can be–

1. Presentation - It can be oral, visual and video. Create, deliver clearly and confidently. Initially, to gain confidence, you can deliver in a closed room and correct your feelings where you need to amend it.

2. Facilitation - Know how to engage, manage, direct people and the team.

3. Communication with clarity, precision and influence will make the delivery highly acceptable.

4. Creativity - To handle a situation on the spot, use creativity.

5. Measuring results from training - Identify and measure the different results of the training.

6. Active listening - Listen in a way to understand and respond suitably.

7. Training of employees is essential for any organization.

8. Public speaking - Speak to the audience with confidence and control.

9. Continuous learning - Engage in learning continuously with enthusiasm to develop skills further.

10. Organizational skills - Organize tasks to save time and efforts.

11. Time management - Prioritize, set goals and delegate for better productivity.

12. Training for trainers - The grassroots trainers are to be trained periodically to update the new developments in the proposed training area.

13. Training strategies - Develop new strategies such as teaching new skills, or updating trainees on changes in the subject field.

14. Skilled manpower can be hired or developed from the existing employees' group by imparting relevant training. The process of training and upgrading internal candidates who are meritorious and eligible, helps in enhancing both skills and morals of inhouse members.

16

PROBLEM-SOLVING

Problems are everywhere, so are the solutions. Unfortunately, we see more of the problems than solutions.

"Most of the problems in life are because of two reasons:

We act without thinking, or we keep on thinking without acting."

"A problem is a chance for you to do your best."

– Duke Ellington

When you start problem-solving, always bear in mind that a solution is there like--

"Where smoke is there, fire is there,

Where a will is there, the way is there,

Where a problem is there, a solution is there."

Problems will come and go; we must enjoy the challenges just like we enjoy observing tides of the sea waves.

"Obstacles are those frightful things you see when you take your eyes off your goal."

– Henry Ford

For problem-solving, identify the nature of the problem. You cannot remain indecisive as--

"You don't drown by falling in the water; you drown by staying there."

– Edwin Louis Cole

Here are two cases of problems obstructing the success path of a project and solutions found in all adversities:

In a project in Assam, I had the task of moving three reactors across Kalyani river to the site. The heaviest reactor was 376 mt; we were unable to move it. We had a group discussion and took these decisions:

We made a 450 mt load-bearing capacity steel pontoon bridge, tested the bridge with 450 mt steel scrap loaded on a hydraulic trailer, which was moved across the river. Then, the reactor was loaded on the same trailer, moved on the bridge and finally across the river and taken to the site.

To solve such problems, one has to innovate a foolproof solution and then apply it.

With the above reactors, we completed the refinery project. After mechanical completion, the unit was in the commissioning stage. Once the first round of heating of the reactors was over, top covers were opened for inspection, and it was found that all 2700 bubble caps were cracked. It was a big problem because refinery commissioning was impacted. When managers and above were called to the conference room to review it, I saw all of them sitting with their faces looking down. The effect was felt by me as well, but for the problem, a solution had to be there.

I said in a louder tone, "The persons who made the complete refinery can definitely solve the problem." Everybody looked up with fractured smiles. We checked with the supplier in Florence, who required 3 months to supply the caps. After searching, a party was located indigenously, and we got the caps in phases. Finally, the group could complete the job in 21 days, and the reactors were again taken in line.

To overcome such problems, one has to work patiently with motivated and dedicated groups, keeping time in mind, and then the solution would come knocking on your door.

To begin problem-solving, start with divergent thinking to list out problems and then analyse to converge ideas related to the most relevant problem which can be taken up for solutions.

"A problem well stated is a problem half solved."

– John Dewey

"The measure of success is not whether you have a tough problem to deal with, but whether it is the same problem you had last year."

– John Foster Dulles

"One thing is sure. We have to do something to solve the problem. We have to do the best we know how at the moment. If it doesn't turn out right, we can modify it as we go along."

– Franklin D. Roosevelt

Use your creative thinking in selecting a set of probable solutions. Now, select the best workable answer/solution from the set.

Creative problem-solving is a radical, new way of looking at the issue.

Problems requiring creative thinking are open-ended problems which have more than one solution.

Some related quotes:

"Never stop doing your best just because someone does not give you credit."

– Kamari Aka Lyrikal

"Impossible is just an opinion."

— Paulo Coelho

"Pearls do not lie on the seashore. If you want one, you must dive for it."

— A famous Chinese proverb

"The way to get started is to quit talking and begin doing."

— Walt Disney

Sometimes brainstorming is also used for cross-fertilization of ideas.

Here, keep in mind that resistance to change will be there in the execution of the change.

Creative ideas are—

"New and useful. It replaces one conceptual world view by another."

Executives have to make decisions which require creative problem-solving in the following areas:

1. Planning
    i)   Determining the mission of the organization.
    ii) Determining the organizational objectives.
    iii) Identifying strengths and weaknesses.
    iv) Adjusting the organizational behaviour and strategies to competitors' strategies.
    v)   Deciding how to implement a competitive strategy.

2. Organizing
    i)   Decide which job distribution should be within the unit or outside the unit of the organization.
    ii) Grouping of jobs.
    iii) Quantify delegation of jobs and eligibility within groups.

iv) Decide the extent of training of the employees.

3. Leading - Find ways of enhancing productivity in the organization.

   "Productivity is never an accident. It is always the result of a commitment to excellence, intelligent planning and focused effort."

   – Paul J. Meyer

4. Controlling

   i) Decide what system of control is needed.

   ii) Setting standard.

   iii) Review and see why the standards/objectives have not been achieved.

Strategies

Five strategies by Mintzberg

   i) Goal/objective setting

   ii) Analysis of (internal and/or external) actions

   iii) Development of strategic attentiveness

   iv) Implementation

   v) Evaluation

The result of problem-solving ends in financial saving from pennies to millions/billions of dollars, depending on its size and severity.

17

EXECUTIVE

By virtue of position, an executive has to provide leadership to his group of subordinates. S/he has to bring up the productivity level, have a keen eye on minimizing WIP, to maximize delivery, at the same time uses the principle of KISS (keep it simple and straight; some say 'stupid' instead of 'straight'). S/he must have a dedicated team which s/he has to hire or change the working culture of the team in position to improve efficiency.

She/He has to take care of all five functions to achieve goals:

1. Planning
2. Organizing
3. Staffing
4. Directing
5. Controlling

As an executive, while doing the jobs you have to follow procedures, place the work where it belongs, crystallize the activities and finally make it happen.

The differences between executives and group leaders are tabulated below:

Basics	Executives	Group Leaders
Origin	Becomes an executive by virtue of his position	A person becomes a leader by virtue of his personal qualities
Formal rights	Gets formal rights in the organization because of his status	Rights are not available to a union leader
Followers	Subordinates are the followers	The group being led is the follower
Necessity	Very essential to a concern	On a voluntary basis, creates a relationship between the group and the organization
Stability	More	Less
Mutual relationship	All executives are leaders	All leaders are not executives
Accountability	To self and subordinates' behaviour and performances	No well-defined accountability
Concern	Organizational goals	Group goals and members' satisfaction
Role constitution	Is in the office till completion of the assignment	Can maintain the position through day-to-day wishes of his followers
Sanctions	Has command over allocation and distribution of sanctions	Concern of related sanctions and task records are essentially of formal nature

An executive has to create a bankable employees' group by building his team. Keep in mind that behind every complaint, there is an unexpected question. Even a benign remark by an employee provides insight into that employee's world.

In your team, do not include such employees who say--

I do not know.

I have not operated in the manner you are saying.

I do not believe what you did.

I do not have time.

Skills that every executive needs:

- Leadership
- Subject-specific skills
- Change management
- Commercial acumen
- Communication
- Strategic thinking
- Decision-making
- Transparency in his work
- Respecting emotions of the group

Further differences in qualities of the two are:

Executive	Group Leader
Maintains	Develops
Focus on systems and structures	Focus on people and their emotions
Controls system and people	Inspires people
Accepts the way things are	Challenges the way things are
Has a short-range view	Has a long-range perspective
Manages tasks	Leads people
Role is administrative	Role is innovative

"For the creation of a leader from a manager/executive, in brief, the following changes are needed:

i) Specialist to generalist - Shift from leading a single function to overseeing a full set of business functions.

ii) Tactician to strategist - Shift day-to-day level of thinking to thinkers, analysers, recognize patterns and construct mental models.

iii) Analyst to integrator - To manage and integrate the collective knowledge of concerned functional teams to solve important organizational problems.

iv) Bricklayer to architect - They have to move to architect level for their organization, its strategy, structure, processes and skill bases.

v) Problem solver to agenda setter - Not only a problem solver but an enterprise leader who defines problems that the organization shall be taking up for solutions.

vi) Warrior to diplomat - Participates in negotiation, persuasion, conflict management and alliance building.

vii) Supporting cast member to lead role - Have to move to centre stage in all important circumstances."

(Refer to Harvard Business Review, 'How Managers Become Leaders', by Michael D. Watkins, Jan 2012 issue)

Another important role for executives, in their status, is to innovate and create new products and services and for this, they have to:

- Link innovation in their strategic plan.

- Create focus, engagement and passion for innovation.

- Allocate fund, resources to this plan.

- Advertise products and services as new development items of superior grades.

- Make a sustainable plan of execution of the innovated ideas.

- Take personal control for implementation of new ideas.

It is a proven fact that most of the inputs from internal innovations which have been implemented have provided high tech projects/products/services at a large profit for the growth of an organization.

Any executive who aspires to be tomorrow's leader has to bear in mind the above points, implement these during the progress of assignments in his/her career to achieve the target.

18

LEADER

A leader--

(L) leads

(E) everyone in his team

(A) and

(D) directs

(E) each member (through his group heads) to move on the

(R) right path of success

Leadership is an art of motivating a group of people to act towards a common goal in a business setting.

The true work of a leader is the willingness to stick with a bold course of action, an unconventional business strategy, a unique product development roadmap, a controversial marketing campaign, even if the rest of the world wonders why he/she is not marching in the step of status quo.

Real leaders are happy to adopt a difficult path while others prefer a straight run. They understand that in an era of intense competition and non-stop disruptions, the only way to stand out from the crowd is to stand for something special.

In his book 'Management in 10 Words', Terry Leahy has summarized the following 10 words for a leader to practice:

1. Truth – It is crucial both to create and to sustain success.

2. Loyalty - Winning and retaining loyalty is the best objective of any business.

   "You reward the behaviour you seek from others."

3. Courage - Good strategies need to be bold and daring. People need to be stretched, as they can do more than they think.

4. Value - Strong values underpin successful businesses, govern how a business behaves, what it sees as important, what it does when faced with problems.

5. Act - Intention is never enough. Plans mean nothing if they are not effectively enacted.

6. Balance - A balanced organization is one in which everyone moves forward together, steered in the right direction without being overrun by the juggernaut of bureaucracy.

7. Simple - Make things simple to face fast-growing company requirements.

8. Lean - Sustainable consumption depends on desiring goods and services that use fewer natural resources. Do more for less.

9. Compete - Do not wait for your competitors to come over the horizon. Seek them out.

10. Trust - When people trust you, they feel that their interests are safe in your hands, and they have confidence in your vision, ability, judgement, drive and determination to see things through.

    "Leaders are problem solvers by talent and temperament, and by choice. For them, the new information environment—

undermining old means of control, opening up old closets of secrecy, reducing the relevance of ownership, early arrival, and location—should seem less a litany of problems than an agenda for action."

– Harlan Cleveland

People have given a number of adjectives to leaders depending upon their LEADERSHIP STYLES, which are:-

1. Transactional - Focus on organization, supervision and group performance.

2. Transformational - Focus on change for betterment within the organization.

3. Authoritarian - Directive behaviour, decides alone, focuses on tasks, does not take meaningful input from the employees.

4. Democratic - Open communication, team leader, focus on people.

5. Bureaucratic - Insecure, knows the rules, impersonal.

6. Participative - Consults group in decision-making, retains final verdict.

7. Delegative - Power basically handed over to the group, useful in highly skilled subordinates' team.

8. Charismatic - Is useful when the organization is in crisis, stress or is changing.

9. Laissez-Faire - Lets them (people's body) *do* as they *will*.

A leader believes in action terminating in success.

"The pessimist complains about the wind.
The optimist expects it to change.
The leader adjusts the sails."

— John Maxwell

In case there is no wind:

"If there is no wind, row."

— Latin proverb

"Be the change you want to see in the world."

— Mahatma Gandhi

A leader never embraces loss, as—

"I never lose, either I win or learn."

— Nelson Mandela

A leader follows the principle of marching ahead--

"Go the extra mile. It is never crowded there."

— Dr Wayne D. Dyer

"The very essence of leadership is that you have to have vision. You can't blow an uncertain trumpet."

— Theodore M. Hesburgh

Humility is an essential part of leadership.

A leader is a person who believes in:

"Do not find fault; find a remedy."

— Henry Ford

"Successful leaders see the opportunities in every difficulty rather than the difficulty in every opportunity."

— Reed Markham

"Leadership and learning are indispensable to each other."
— John F. Kennedy

"If your actions inspire others to dream more, learn more, do more and become more, you are a leader."
— John Quincy Adams

Remember that:

"Management is doing things right, but leadership is doing the right things."
— Peter F. Drucker

Another important skill that leaders have is innovation.

"Innovation distinguishes a leader and a follower."
— Steve Jobs, Apple Inc.

Leadership is the ability to get extraordinary achievements from ordinary people.

His/her efforts are always focused, as you know that—

"When you require fire, the sun's rays do not burn until brought to a focus."

When you want to bring up your followers, and the environment around is rough, you have to keep in mind occasionally that--

"A smooth sea can never make a skilled sailor."

You also have to think that—

"If leadership is liked always, then it will be a friendship."

"As a leader, you must have clarity, humility and courage. Ensure humility sticks with you always like a glue."
— Deepak Parekh

A leader uses intelligence, maturity, personality and his/her leadership in situation-bound circumstances.

He/she is required at all levels. At the top level, they get cooperation in terms of plans and policies. At the middle and lower levels, they are required to interpret and execute plans and programmes framed by the management. He/she is the representative of the organization.

He/she integrates and reconciles personal goals with organizational goals. He/she can solicit support and is an essential part of management, and leadership is a potential in them to influence and drive the group efforts towards achieving the goal. He/she sets strategies that build and sustain competitive advantages.

A leader is a person who commands a group, an organization or a country. Sometimes, leaders are made by circumstances.

Top five basic qualities of a leader are:

i) Clarity - Clear and concise at all times, which leads to great achievement.

ii) Decisiveness - Consistent in decisions and commitments.

iii) Courage - Can develop boldness; for some, it is a blessed virtue.

iv) Passion - As long as he is passionate about what he knows and cares about, it will shine through and people will follow.

v) Humility - Humble character for creating a lovable persona. He accepts critique and reforms himself with gratitude.

Some more virtues of a leader are:

i) A pleasing appearance.

ii) Good vision, foresight, intelligence.

iii) Good communicator.

iv) His objectivity is free from bias.

v) His judgement is based on facts and logic.

vi) Can assess knowledge of work for himself and his subordinates so that he can win their trust and confidence.

vii) Has a high sense of responsibility.

viii) His self-confidence and will power are strong and trustworthy.

ix) Treats his subordinates on humanitarian grounds.

x) His empathy is always ready to step into others' shoes, and he has personal contact with them.

Briefly, leadership skills are:

i) Strategic thinking

ii) Planning and guidance in delivery

iii) People management skills

iv) Change in management and innovations

v) Communication

vi) Coaching

With the above skills, a leader always makes his followers into a team because individual talents win games, but teamwork wins championships.

CONCLUSION

I have brought all of your needs to one place.

You have gone through several supporting threads (SUTRAs) of life from the 1ˢᵗ to 18ᵗʰ chapters.

You may like to adopt a few of them in your career and day-to-day working environments, which will guide you to smooth sailing through your journey. Your performance will be enhanced, and your advancement will be on a changed track.

This book provides proven advice to aspiring students/beginners on the management ladder/executives and leaders.

I wish for your success, which will give me enjoyment.